Nature's Underground Wonderland

KARTCHNER

CAVERNS

STATE PARK® By Sam Negri

Photographs copyrighted by Arizona State Parks are by K.L. Day and Arizona Conservation Projects. Additional photography by David Elms and Noelle Wilson.

Russ Wall and Barbara Denney — Designers
Kevin Kibsey — Map Illustration
Annette Phares — Production Assistant

Bonnie Trenga and Betty Campbell — Copy Editors
Richard Maack — Photography Editor
Robert J. Farrell and Evelyn Howell — Book Editors

Prepared by the Book Division of *Arizona Highways* in cooperation with Arizona State Parks.

Win Holden — Publisher
Bob Albano — Managing Editor
Evelyn Howell — Associate Editor
PK Perkin McMahon — Associate Editor

Kim Ensenberger — Production Director
Peter Ensenberger — Director of Photography

Printed in the United States.   Library of Congress Catalog Number 97-76032   ISBN 1-893860-20-5

(COVER) This collage shows some of Kartchner's hanging stalactites overlaid by a site diagram of the cave. The diagram motif is repeated throughout the book.

(INSIDE FRONT COVER) Framed by rising stalagmites and icicle-like stalactites, a flowstone formation in the **Big Room** looks like a melting wedding cake. Kartchner Caverns is a significant find because it is a "living" cave — these mineral formations are still growing with each tiny drip of water.

(ABOVE) Nestled in southeastern Arizona's Whetstone Mountains, the Discovery Center, which includes exhibits and a Kartchner Caverns film for visitors, blends into its environment.

(BACK COVER) Kubla Khan, the large central column, dwarfs an observer in the Throne Room. Almost 60 feet high, Kubla Khan is the highest known column in an Arizona cave.

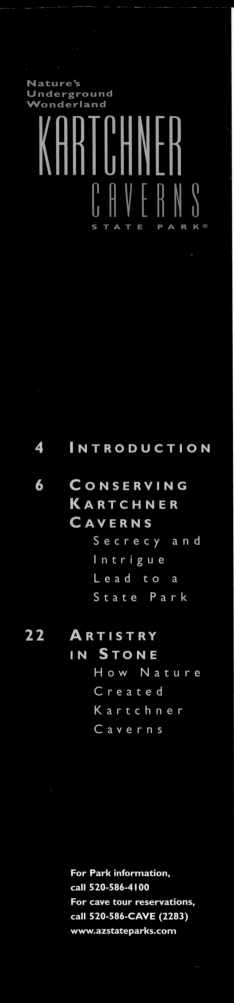

Nature's
Underground
Wonderland

KARTCHNER
CAVERNS
STATE PARK®

For Park information,
call 520-586-4100
For cave tour reservations,
call 520-586-CAVE (2283)
www.azstateparks.com

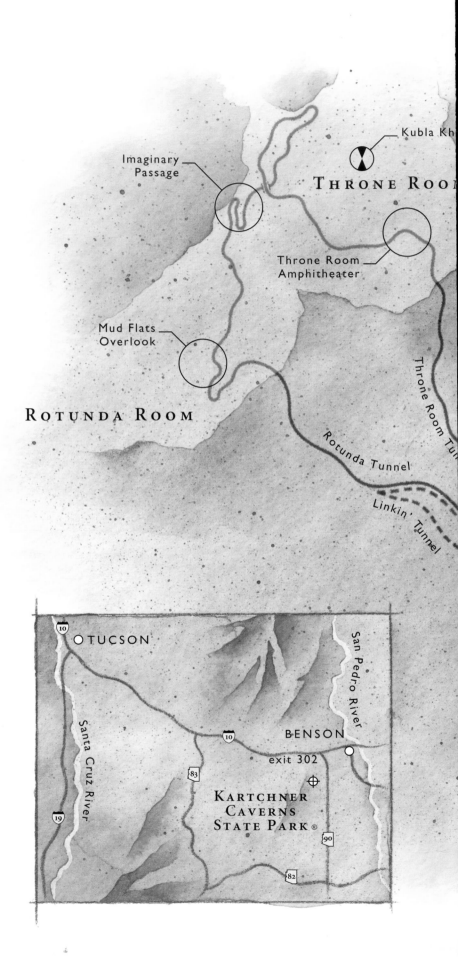

Kubla Kh

Imaginary
Passage

THRONE ROO

Throne Room
Amphitheater

Mud Flats
Overlook

ROTUNDA ROOM

Throne Room Tunn

Rotunda Tunnel

Linkin' Tunnel

TUCSON

San Pedro River

BENSON

exit 302

Santa Cruz River

KARTCHNER
CAVERNS
STATE PARK®

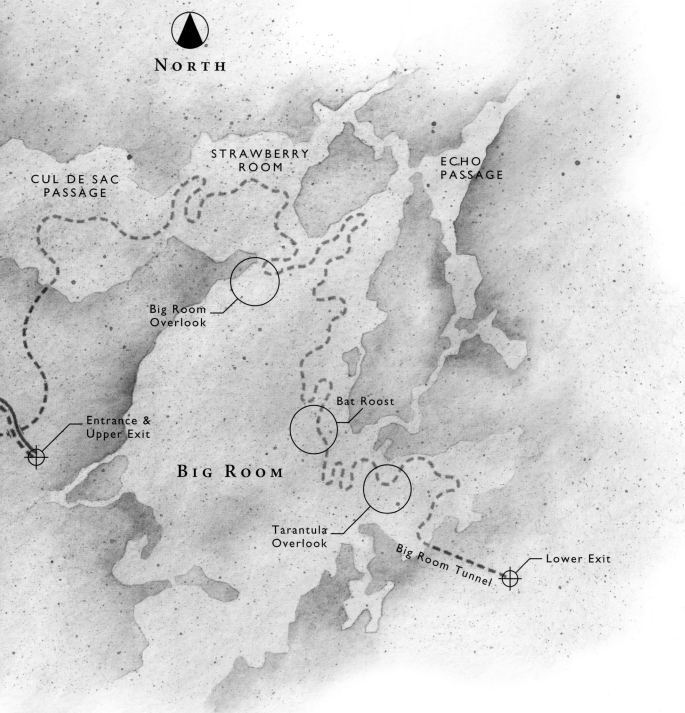

ROTUNDA/THRONE ROOM TOUR

BIG ROOM TOUR
See Tour Information on Page 32

NORTH

CUL DE SAC
PASSAGE

STRAWBERRY
ROOM

ECHO
PASSAGE

Big Room
Overlook

Bat Roost

Entrance &
Upper Exit

BIG ROOM

Tarantula
Overlook

Big Room Tunnel

Lower Exit

INTRODUCTION

Kartchner Caverns State Park® opened to the public on November 12, 1999. Such a simple statement that is, but it took us years to be able to say it. Years of secrecy, excitement, struggle, and bafflement. Cave experts, park rangers, geologists, construction crews, bat biologists, legislators — all of us working as a team on a monumental project, the likes of which few had ever tackled before. The initial opening brought the Throne and Rotunda rooms to public view; in November 2003, we opened the Big Room. Now that it's been 30 years since the dramatic saga of Kartchner Caverns began, and the cave is considered one of the world's 10 most colorful and varied limestone caverns, I sometime take time to think back . . .

. . . I got up on the morning of my second trip into Kartchner Caverns feeling as though it was my birthday. It was that happy feeling that gifts await you just for being there. It made me smile, and I was still smiling as a group of us milled around the cave entrance.

When Randy Tufts [who died in 2002] and Gary Tenen first ventured into the cave in 1974, there were no human footprints. Imagine. There were footprints on the moon before there were footprints in Kartchner.

Kartchner Caverns, in southern Arizona, was named after the family who owned the land and helped protect the cave. Below the desert landscape, Kartchner has all the ingredients of a subtropical rain forest except the most important: the light of the sun.

Basic chemical reactions have been the architect of this underground landscape. Those reactions that first hollowed out the limestone base are still filling it with stalactites, "soda straws," and calcite "shields," still staining the walls with mineral tapestries of reds, blue-greens, browns, grays, and whites.

Before we went "down under" on my second trip, park rangers reminded us of procedures to protect not only ourselves but also delicate cave features, some so fragile that a careless touch could ruin thousands of years of growth.

We made our way down the 40-foot-long shaft and entered Kartchner through an air-lock door. A short crawl through the first chamber and we stood up in the "big room."

Nearby, shadows hid behind stalactites as we moved by with our headlamps. The bobbing of our heads as we walked made the shadows dance. Yet just a short distance beyond was complete, solid darkness. Our light was absorbed by the void, and what might have been a hundred yards to the outer wall could just as well have been a hundred miles.

Because Kartchner's humidity is almost 100 percent and the temperature is a steady 68° F just below the surface of the desert, we knew we'd need to ensure that the cave didn't dry out when we opened it to the public. Dry air would halt the essential chemical reactions still at work in the cave.

Lighting the cave would be particularly tricky. Microscopic spores would enter on people's clothing, and the lights added along the paths could trigger their growth in the humid conditions, with untold results. Keep the lights too low, however, and visitors would stumble dangerously.

(ABOVE)
A heavy calcite shield looms over rounded stalagmites.

How would we get people close enough to the formations so they could fully appreciate their beauty, but not so close

Photography by K.L. Day and Arizona Conservation Projects (page 4 and page 5, bottom) and David Elms (page 5, top).

that a curious hand would damage them?

The list of issues seemed endless. How would we protect the small colony of bats that roost in Kartchner during the summer? How large should a group tour be, and how long should a tour take, without threatening the subterranean ecosystem? Could we develop cave trails without stairs that would allow complete access for the disabled visitor?

As we made our way back to the entrance shaft, we slowed, partly because crawling and stooping for the last four hours in an atmosphere of 100 percent humidity was taking its toll. But also, we didn't want to leave — there might be one more beautifully sculpted stalactite or helictite that we didn't want to miss.

In the time since that second trip, I was to find that the technical challenges of developing Kartchner Caverns were every bit as complex as we'd anticipated — and then some. Sometimes, those challenges seemed more like frustrations, but I've had the privilege of working with a dedicated team that never gave up. With Randy Tufts, Gary Tenen, and the Kartchner family, we dreamed of the world being able to stand in stunned awe and marvel at what we were seeing that day. That dream has come true.

I recall a hunting trip with my grandfather when I was young. Alone for a while, I found a large English walnut tree to sit under and, thinking youthful thoughts, wondered if anyone had ever sat there before. Looking down, I saw a discarded tin can. I had wondered ever since if there were any place left on Earth that man hadn't ruined with disrespect. Kartchner Caverns is such a place.

KEN TRAVOUS
DIRECTOR, ARIZONA
STATE PARKS

Spelunkers Randy Tufts, left, and Gary Tenen discovered Kartchner Caverns in 1974.

IN MEMORIAM

RANDY TUFTS, 1948-2002

Explorer, scientist, thinker; good friend to many, kind and caring to everyone. — *Gary Tenen*

SECRECY AND INTRIGUE LEAD TO A STATE PARK

James Kartchner may have been the first to notice something a bit unusual about the hills above the cave that now bears his name. Kartchner was an educator and a rancher in St. David, a small town east of the Whetstone Mountains, in southeastern Arizona. Whenever he and his sons would ride the hills to check on their cattle, their horses' hoofs made a peculiar sound on the limestone rock. "You know," Kartchner commented to his sons, "it sounds like these hills are hollow."

He'd bought land in the Whetstones, about 40 miles southeast of Tucson, in 1942. It would be another 32 years before anyone would find just how hollow the hills were.

Various spelunkers had poked around the Whetstones hoping to find a new cave.

(ABOVE) This "butterscotch" formation hangs in the Rotunda Room like a translucent wave of toffee being pulled by a confectioner.

These amateur cave explorers look for certain clues. An area with limestone may also contain caves since limestone dissolves when water seeps through it, forming underground cavities. Sinkholes are another good sign. A sinkhole is a depression in the ground created when these cavities collapse. The Whetstones have the most extensive limestone deposits in southern Arizona and are riddled with sinkholes. But until 1974, no one had ever found a cave worth talking about. Or, as we shall see, worth *not* talking about.

In 1966, Randy Tufts, a Tucson native with an insatiable curiosity about caves, started making regular trips to the Whetstone Mountains looking, as he put it, "for a cave no one had ever found." At that time one of the few decent roads into the Whetstones went up Middle Canyon, passing the Lone

Photography by Noelle Wilson (page 6) and K.L. Day and Arizona Conservation Projects (page 7).

Part of the Big Room,
the jagged ceiling and spiked
floor shown here are a fraction
of an area that is about as long
as a football field.

Water droplets bead the tips of translucent rock tubes called "soda straws." The larger, surrounding stalactites, nicknamed "carrots," formed when soda straws clogged, and the mineralized solution poured down the sides.

Photography by David Elms (page 8 and page 9, bottom) and K.L. Day and Arizona Conservation Projects (page 9, top, and pages 10-11).

Star fluorite mine, located in the Coronado National Forest directly west of the Kartchners' property. After about a dozen trips into the range, Tufts had met with little success. Finally, out of frustration he stopped at the Lone Star Mine and asked one of the miners if he knew of any caves in the area. The miner said yes, there was a cave nearby.

"Some high school kids got into it. They had to squeeze through a tight spot to do it," he said. According to the miner, the cave was located somewhere in the limestone knolls that Tufts had been driving by each time he went exploring in the Whetstones.

Tufts returned with two friends and his uncle. They hiked around the limestone knolls and eventually found a sinkhole and an opening that led into a small chamber. There was a narrow crack along one wall, and they looked to see if it might lead deeper in. They could determine nothing and, feeling the boulders near the crack were unstable, decided to leave. The chamber must be just another dusty dry hole that wasn't worth pursuing. However,

(BELOW) Interested hikers may explore the Whetstone Mountains on adjacent national forest land. A trailhead starts in Kartchner Caverns State Park.

Tufts marked the hole on his topographic map.

For the next seven years, he was too absorbed studying geology at the University of Arizona to do much caving. In 1970, he became friends with Gary Tenen, and they worked together at a coffeehouse. A

year later, still students, the two moved into an apartment with a mutual friend.

Tenen knew of Tufts' interest in caving, but he had never tried it. Because of his own interest in science — he was an entomology student —

(ABOVE) Facing the Dragoon Mountains to the east, the Discovery Center offers exhibits and a Kartchner Caverns film for visitors.

he asked Tufts to take him on one of his caving excursions. Their first trip was to a cave in the Huachuca Mountains, south of the Whetstones, and even though it was a heavily vandalized cave, the experience was enough to whet Tenen's appetite for caving. His enthusiasm rekindled Tufts' interest in caving, and before long the two were out scouring the vacant hills south and east of Tucson.

In the fall of 1974, Tufts went back to the Whetstones with another friend, a non-caver. He quickly found the sinkhole that he had marked earlier. However, this time, walking near a stream on the southern side of the hill, they found a horizontal hole some 60 yards from the sinkhole. Tufts wondered if a cave passage connected the two openings. He told Tenen about his theory, and the two agreed to explore the next weekend.

On a cool November afternoon, they went back. First they explored the horizontal entrance, but

This view is into the immense Big Room with its forest of stalactites. The reddish formation above the observer's right shoulder is "cave bacon," colored by deposits of iron oxide.

concluded that major excavation would be needed to get into it any deeper than 30 feet. They then looked at the opening on the other side, in the sinkhole, even though Tufts had found nothing seven years earlier. They squirmed into the chamber, and Tufts said that, although everything looked much as he remembered it, something seemed different.

"This time the air was moving," Tufts said. "There was a breeze coming up from between the rocks, through a crack. Not just any breeze. It was warm, moist, and smelled like bat guano. This was new and compelling evidence."

The fact that it was a cool November day no doubt made a difference. On the previous trip, he hadn't felt the warm breeze from the cave because he had been there in warmer weather.

"The cave wasn't breathing," he observed.

The two twisted their way down through the crack. Five feet below, and not visible from above, was a chamber about the size of an average living room. They saw unmistakable evidence — footprints and broken stalactites — that others had been this far before. A crawl space led to a second small room. But neither room was large enough to account for the breeze. Only a sizable cave could produce it, but where was it coming from?

After inspecting the two rooms, they discovered a crawlway at floor level in the second room. It was about 10 inches high and 2 feet across. The breeze came from that hole. Tufts squirmed in, inching forward about 20 feet until the tunnel abruptly ended against a rock barrier. However, in the middle of the barrier there was a 6-inch oval-shaped hole through which a damp wind blew. Tufts tried to peer through the opening, but the wind kept blowing out his carbide light.

This was the kind of moment that stirs a caver's blood. Something was definitely behind that small fissure. Cavers often ask when they find a new passage, "Does it go?" meaning, does this lead anywhere or will it be another dead end? Clearly, this hole went someplace, but where? With the thrill of discovery propelling them, Tufts and Tenen went

(ABOVE) A mud-soaked caver enters the Throne Room. Before a tunnel was created connecting it and the Big Room, cave workers spent two to three hours moving from one room to the other to go about research and other tasks. In places, they went on all fours through cold mud and sometimes water.

(BELOW LEFT) A calcite shield is fluted with mineral draperies.
(BELOW RIGHT) A member of the cave-development team
examines a ceiling spiked with stalactites. Glistening with
moisture, the rounded formations beside him are rocky debris
covered with flowstone made of minerals deposited by water.

Photography by K.L. Day and Arizona Conservation Projects (pages 12-13, top, and page 13, bottom) and David Elms (page 12, bottom).

to work with an 8-pound sledgehammer, taking turns chipping away at the limestone bedrock until the hole was barely large enough for a person to squeeze through.

Tenen, the smaller of the two, is 5 feet 7 inches tall and then weighed 130 pounds. He'd practiced for tight spots like this one by wiggling through ordinary coat hangers. Tufts, who was 6 feet tall and weighed 170 pounds, had to remove his shirt and exhale to make it through the opening. "It was like being born all over again," he remarked.

After the blowhole, the passage became slightly higher. They were able to crawl on hands and knees on a floor carpeted with bat guano and hackberry seeds. There was no sign on the walls or the floor that any human being had ever been there. Some 50 feet ahead of them they could see only darkness. They crawled toward that space and found themselves in a 10-foot-high corridor that took off in two directions. They were able to walk upright for the next 300 feet. Around them, in the jerky light of their headlamps, the chamber glistened with stalactites, soda straws (stalactites the thickness of a drinking straw), and tiny twisted fingers of calcite called helictites. They walked gingerly, taking care not to touch or damage anything.

They continued a bit farther, but neither knew how far they had gone. What they did know was that they had violated a prime rule of caving. They had not told anyone of their whereabouts. Cavers typically leave information with someone at home, and almost always they travel in fours. If someone is in trouble, one can stay with the injured person and two can go for help. Tufts and Tenen were on their own. They could have been buried alive and no one would ever know what had become of them.

It was a sobering thought, so they stopped and carefully retraced their steps, giddy with the thrill of the amazing world they had stumbled into. It was every caver's dream: an untouched, living cave, elaborately decorated with formations that were still growing. It was a subterranean jewel box that had taken about a million years to form, and no other humans had ever set foot inside it.

Tufts was born in 1948; Tenen in 1951. In 1974, they were still young men, and suddenly they were young men with a problem. They had done enough caving in southern Arizona to know that once word of a new find slipped out, hordes of curious individuals would descend on the cave. Before long, the great untouched gallery would be destroyed by graffiti and litter, desecrated by souvenir hunters taking home bits of stalactites and other formations that had been growing in the darkness for a million years.

Making matters worse, the cave was too accessible. It was only a half-mile off a paved state route and a mere 8 miles south of a major interstate highway. From the cave's entrance, traffic could be heard clearly.

They believed that, since they had found the cave, they should protect it. But what were they to do? For safety's sake and to avoid the inevitable publicity if a public rescue were necessary, they had to bring others into the picture. At first, these were a few friends who were athletic but not cavers and thus unlikely to return on their own. One was their roommate, Steve Northway, who provided the cave's first name. Northway couldn't fit into the first crack to get into the cave, so he sat outside. When the others emerged, he suggested they call the place "Xanadu," the terrestrial paradise Samuel Taylor Coleridge invented in his famous poem, *Kubla Khan*: "In Xanadu did Kubla Khan / A stately pleasure-dome decree..."

It took a full year of exploration before Tufts and Tenen knew the full extent of what they had discovered. What they had crawled into that November day turned out to be the entrance to a cave 2-and-a-half miles long, containing two large rooms. If the "breakdown" or fallen rock were removed, each room would be roughly the size of a football field. Off the two main rooms were 26 smaller ones, almost all of them dripping with eerie, elaborate rock formations.

To preserve the cave, they marked their trails and placed many areas off-limits. They took care not to touch anything. If they accidentally broke a formation, they glued it back together with dental cement. Not wanting to leave footprints in some sensitive passages, they removed their shoes and walked in

Rock formations decorate a curve of ceiling only where faults and fissures in the stone allow water to seep through, building the tiny soda straws and draping the mounded column with dissolved limestone.

their socks. "We did not treat Xanadu as a recreational cave," Tenen noted. "Once we concluded we had found all of it, we stopped going."

A few friends and cavers knew what they had found, though all were sworn to secrecy. Numerous relatives and friends were simply not told. The guiding principle was that only those "who needed to know" for safety's sake, or to continue exploration, would be told. When dealing with strangers, they adopted aliases for themselves and deliberately steered attention away from the Whetstones.

After the initial burst of exhilaration over their find, Tufts and Tenen were in a quandary. How could they keep such an accessible cave secret and pristine? Inevitably, someone else would discover

Photography by David Elms (page 14 and pages 16-17) and K.L. Day and Arizona Conservation Projects (page 15).

it. After much thought, they settled on what Tufts called "a paradoxical notion": Why not protect the cave by developing it as a commercial attraction?

In 1977, Tufts visited various developed caves to see how Xanadu compared. He told Tenen that it was as good as or better than other tourist caves. "We thought if it had economic value, someone would supervise it and protect it," Tenen said. They considered buying the land and developing the cave themselves, but neither had the money.

At first, they didn't know the cave was on private land — an easy mistake to make in Arizona, where hills and mountains are often a mosaic of state, federal, and private land. They soon learned James and Lois

In the Strawberry Room, the color of these formations is from iron oxide. To the left is the shoulder of a large formation nicknamed "Strawberry Shortcake."

Kartchner of St. David owned the land. But who were the Kartchners and what were they like?

In the many years since 1978, when Tufts and Tenen approached James Kartchner in his front yard, they have repeatedly commented on the cave's good fortune. Kartchner, who died in 1986, had been a science teacher and the superintendent of schools in St. David. He and Lois had 10 children of their own and two that they adopted. Six of their children are medical doctors, and one had a Ph.D.

Tenen, an avid photographer, had taken numerous slides of the cave's formations. He and Tufts had prepared a script and planned to divulge their find gradually, only after they had gauged the Kartchners' attitude. They quickly realized James Kartchner was at least as interested in geology and related matters as they were, and the script went out the window. Tenen set up his slides, cautioning his host about the need for secrecy.

Soon after, when Kartchner was 78, he and five of his sons accompanied Tufts and Tenen on a cave tour to determine its potential for development. The discoverers hoped the family would see the need for protection. They needn't have worried.

"We were in complete disbelief at the size and beauty of it," said Max Kartchner, an anesthesiologist who lives in Benson. "It was almost a sacred experience, so exquisite and out of this world."

After seeing the cave, the family asked Tufts and Tenen to prepare a proposal outlining the best options for protecting it. The two then set out to learn as much as they could about how trails and lighting could be installed in a cave without damaging it. Using money from a joint bank account they had set up with the Kartchners, and determined to maintain secrecy, they adopted new aliases and hired Jan and Orion Knox, a couple from Austin, Texas, to map the cave.

Tenen went by "Mike Lewis," Tufts by "Bob Clark." An amusing coincidence, they realized later, that their new names were Lewis and Clark, like the two explorers who had made the scientific survey of much of western North America from 1803 to 1806.

Tenen used his alias when he attended two conventions of the National Caves Association and when he worked for five months as a volunteer at Caverns

Near the main trail, the ceiling's arch opens into the Big Room, where the roof peaks at 55 feet. The ceiling in the Throne Room, Kartchner's other large chamber, reaches about 70 feet at its highest point.

of Sonora in Texas and at Luray Caverns in Virginia. He paid for everything with cash to avoid using checks or credit cards that showed his real name.

The elaborate ruse was necessary because the national caving community was tight-knit. Information and rumors could spread rapidly. Since cavers sometimes become identified with mountain ranges they explored, Tufts and Tenen feared that if they used their real names, the word would get out that they had found something in the Whetstones. Anyone they told about the cave, except the Kartchners and, later, Bruce Babbitt, then governor of Arizona, was required to sign a secrecy agreement, threatening "theological punishment" to anyone who divulged the cave's location or even its existence.

Still, leaks occurred. One led to a scene that could have come straight out of an old Western movie. Steve Holland, a caver and acquaintance of Tenen, overheard a group planning a trip to the Whetstones to search for a rumored cave on the Kartchner land. He informed Tenen, and they devised a plan. Holland would wrangle an invitation to go along with the other four cavers. "I became a mole," he said. He told Tenen when the group was going to be at the cave. Tenen contacted the Kartchners to arrange a confrontation that would scare off the interlopers.

A few months later, the five cavers showed up at the site to excavate the horizontal entrance that Tufts and Tenen had originally abandoned as impenetrable. Minutes after their arrival, three Kartchner brothers, Paul, Rex, and Fred, rode up on horseback, one with a pistol dangling from his side. "What are you doing on our land?" one of them asked the group.

Holland pretended to be as shocked as the other cavers. "The Kartchners acted like rough and tough ranchers, even though one of them was an anesthesiologist and another a teacher," he recalled. They took down the names of the interlopers, told them they were trespassing, and warned them they would be arrested if they were ever found there again.

Eventually, the Kartchners decided the cost of developing the cave themselves was prohibitive.

(ABOVE) A close-up look at some rootlike helictites. Appearing almost fibrous, they are hardened mineral like all the cave formations. (RIGHT) Tightly clustered stalactites hover over blockier stalagmites.

However, along with Tufts and Tenen, they continued to guard the cave. Finally, in 1984, Tufts and Tenen proposed an alternative: Maybe the state would be interested in purchasing the site to develop it as a state park.

The discoverers approached then-Governor Bruce Babbitt. He was interested, but wanted to see the cave for himself. Babbitt, who had a background in geology before he became a lawyer, toured the cave in April 1985. He brought along his sons, Chris, 10, and T.J., 8, first making them promise they would keep it a secret. He also lectured them on not touching anything and following directions carefully.

"After this great lecture, the only person who knocked over a stalagmite was me," the governor said. "We were climbing up an incline, and my heel knocked over a baby stalagmite. My kids have never let me forget it."

Impressed, Babbitt threw his support behind the clandestine movement to get the cave into public ownership. One of the biggest problems involved obtaining an appraisal of the property and guiding the project through the legislative process without attracting publicity and jeopardizing the site.

It took three more years, two more governors, two more state parks directors, and some tense, behind-the-scenes political maneuvering before the state bought the cave. Everyone involved was so consumed

Photography by K.L. Day and Arizona Conservation Projects (both pages).

(ABOVE) Like medieval tapestries hanging in a true castle's throne room, these stone draperies add a regal touch to Kartchner's Throne Room. (LEFT) Crouched beneath a stony vault, a worker looks at a backlit slab of "cave bacon." The corrugated upright spire is a stalagmite.

with the need for secrecy that State Parks Director Ken Travous asked state legislative leaders to write the bill authorizing the cave's purchase in obscure language so that no one would know what was at stake until the vote. Essentially dummy legislation, Senate Bill 1188 made no mention of the cave. Its original wording covered routine accounting changes within the parks department. Until the final vote, only six legislators knew that this particular legislation actually authorized the state to buy the cave and the land around it for $1,625,000.

The day the bill was passed, April 27, 1988, its language was changed to clearly establish what now is Kartchner Caverns State Park®. The State Senate approved the measure by a vote of 27-0; the House by 52-4. After 14 years of protective secrecy, the cave and the new park were announced to the public.

While the cave's discovery and the elaborate secrecy were remarkable, the steps that followed were just as significant to Kartchner's future. Travous assembled a team of respected cavern experts to study everything in the cave and everything outside that might impact the interior. Ron Bridgemon, former president of the Cave Research Foundation, an organization that studies caves throughout the United States, said that, to his knowledge, no scientific studies before had been done prior to developing a cave as a tourist attraction.

"These studies are usually done after the cave has opened [to the public] and something has been messed up," he said. "Then they go back in and try to fix it. What the state [has done] with Kartchner is unique."

In addition, experts in designing cave tours were recruited to supervise the underground construction and development. Extraordinary care was taken in the development, both above and below ground, to keep the cave in good condition.

Kartchner Caverns became a state park so that it could be preserved and protected and used as a living classroom where the public could learn something about earth sciences and the fragile life of a cave environment. For Tufts and Tenen, the creation of the park was like an investment from which all other caves might profit once the public saw its remarkable features and learned the necessity of preserving it and other caves for future generations.

(BELOW) A set of small "fried eggs" cluster on the cave floor.

ARTISTRY IN STONE

HOW NATURE CREATED
KARTCHNER CAVERNS

"ook closely. Can you see that droplet of water?"

The speaker was Randy Tufts. Standing in his Tucson living room in November 1996, we were discussing how the cave formations started from a single drop of water. Kartchner Caverns had not yet opened as Arizona's 25th state park.

A photograph showed a cave wall in Kartchner Caverns. It looked like a textured drape with muted colors forming bands that dropped in a more or less diagonal pattern. Tufts pointed to a bright spot that seemed suspended in the blackness to the left of the wall.

The image was not merely a photo of a rock and some moisture, but a picture of a process at work. The tiny

(ABOVE) Looking as appetizing as a real strip of bacon, mineral slabs like this are typically an eighth of an inch thick. (OPPOSITE) In the main passage of the Big Room, a visitor stands in front of ridged draperies capped by flowstone.

droplet in the photo had just fallen from the end of something called a soda straw, a narrow, glass-like tube of rock hanging from the cave's ceiling.

The droplet of water seeped through the limestone, picking up calcium carbonate as it went; when the water hit the air in the cave, a chemical transformation occurred that eventually created the soda straw. The fragile soda straw, if it doesn't break under its own weight or from someone knocking it, will eventually grow into a stalactite, but that process will take thousands of years.

Typically, most stalactites and stalagmites grow only one-tenth of a millimeter per year, which is thinner than a strand of human hair. Having studied the buildup of these calcite deposits on primitive tools found in other caves, scientists estimate it would take more than 750 years to accumulate 1 inch.

Photography by K.L. Day and Arizona Conservation Projects (both pages).

(LEFT) Delicate soda straws build slowly until they break under their own weight. Sticking up from the mud, such fragments have been undisturbed for perhaps 20,000 years.
(ABOVE) Portions of Kartchner Caverns flood periodically, an important natural process for maintaining the cave's humidity. As water recedes, the mud acts as a humidity bank.

Photography by K.L. Day and Arizona Conservation Projects (page 24 and pages 26-27) and David Elms (page 25).

However, 750 years in the life of a rock or a cave is like the blink of an eye compared to the millions of years it takes to prepare for the creation of that single inch. Before there can be a limestone cave, there must be limestone. Where did the limestone come from? What forces created an underground cavern filled with so many exotic shapes and colors? The answers lie millions of years in the past.

Some 200 million years ago, compacted limestone, formed 150 million years earlier from ancient marine life, was propelled upward by the buckling of the earth's crust and occasional volcanoes. These upheavals formed mountains in the inland sea that once covered what is now Arizona. Later, shifts in the tectonic plates under the earth created great cracks and fissures that let water penetrate the limestone deposits in places like the Whetstone Mountains, creating, about one million years ago, the cave now called Kartchner Caverns.

Compared to granite or shale, limestone is a highly soluble rock. As rain falls, it combines with the air's carbon dioxide to form a weak carbonic acid solution, which seeps through millions of cracks in the mountain's surface and dissolves the limestone. In the final stages of this cave's development, the level of the underground water dropped, leaving open chambers in the limestone.

The first drop of water to seep through the mountain's surface soils and reach that ancient cavity began the process of decorating Kartchner Caverns with the stunning variety of calcite formations.

While the shapes and colors of the formations in Kartchner vary considerably, depending on minerals carried in the water and the trajectory of the water, the chemical process is the same. Acidic rainwater seeps underground and when it reaches an air-filled

Soda straws, looking like filaments of spider silk, dangle from the ceiling of the Big Room.

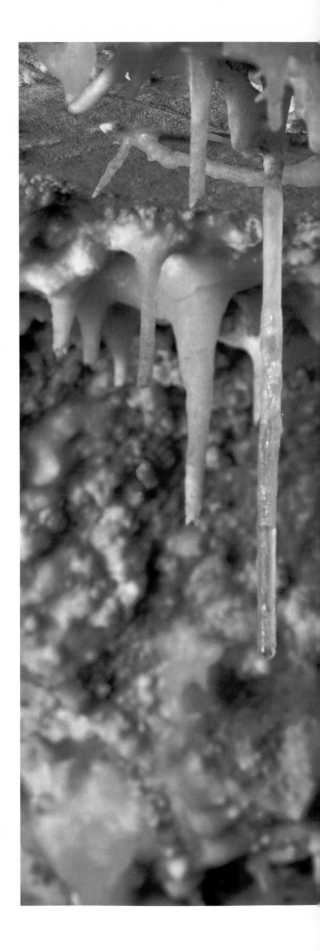

cave, it loses its carbon dioxide and crystallizes into calcium carbonate.

If we could speed up this process enough to watch it happening, we would see that each droplet of water, carrying its load of dissolved minerals, hangs from the ceiling before it drops to the floor. Even in that brief time, some of the carbon dioxide escapes from the water, causing a ring of calcium carbonate to form on the ceiling. Later, another droplet hangs from this spot, and in the same way it adds a layer of mineral to the ring.

After countless years of slow drip after drip, these rings form a hollow, straw-like cylinder. As the cylinder develops, droplets run down the inside as well as the outside and merge at the tip in a formation with the shape of an icicle, known as a stalactite. A similar process occurs on the floor of the cave. When the water droplet splashes on the floor, carbon dioxide escapes, leaving behind — because of the splash — an irregular layer of calcium carbonate, which eventually will grow into rough cylindrical formations. These formations rising from the cave's floor are known as stalagmites.

The process of making the cavity itself takes longer than making the formations, and

(ABOVE) Stark and pale, the Crystal Totem stands in the Throne Room. (RIGHT) Geologists estimate that soda straws grow a tenth of an inch every century, depending on how much outside water seeps in.

Photography by K.L. Day and Arizona Conservation Projects (page 28, top) and David Elms (pages 28-29).

29

(ABOVE) One of many stunning natural arrangements, this titanic duo of column and stalagmite dwarf the man beside them.
(OPPOSITE) It may look like an icy waterfall, but this is a shield of rock. Visitors can spot several shields in the cave, but this one is not on a public trail.

geologists say the interesting thing about a place like Kartchner is that it may not be the final curtain call: Over time there may be changes in the chemistry and the formations, and as a result the formations can keep changing.

Kartchner is an almost pristine example of the whole process. Limestone caves are abundant, but most are inaccessible. The vast majority are also extremely small. One exception is the chamber at Carlsbad Caverns, New Mexico, which is nearly a mile long and 350 feet high.

Throughout Karchner's dizzying network of narrow passageways, elaborate friezes adorn the walls with curled helictites, calcified limestone formed by water forcing its way through tiny fissures. Pale draperies — formed when trickling water deposits an undulating line of calcite on the underside of a sloping ceiling or wall — sometimes

are striped with reddish brown bands (produced by various iron compounds) that look remarkably like large slabs of bacon. In fact these formations are called "cave bacon." Other formations seem to be perfect sunny-side-up eggs.

Like Carlsbad, Kartchner Caverns is home to a population of bats. Between 1,000 and 2,000 insect-eating bats, mostly pregnant females, move into Kartchner's Big Room from May to September and raise their young.

Studies of the bat guano found in the Throne Room — long empty of bats — show that they roosted there some 50,000 years ago. The bats play an important part in the cave's life cycle. Their fertilizing excrement provides nutrients that enable other organisms to grow. These organisms have grown for thousands of years in complete darkness, a vital consideration for preserving the cave's original condition. Park designers, intent on keeping the cave functioning as naturally as possible, chose special lighting that would not encourage the growth of algae or any of the other life forms that might be affected by a change in the light levels.

Kartchner is remarkable because it is a "wet" or "live" cave — the calcite formations are still growing. Though the outside terrain is arid, the cave's relative humidity averages 99 percent all year. And while outside temperatures can reach 100° in the summer,

(BELOW) Mounded flowstone drips over limestone draperies, with tips of stalactites showing in the background.

(RIGHT) A "fried egg" rests on a pedestal.
(BELOW) A visitor enjoys a quiet moment at an overlook in the Big Room.
(OPPOSITE) Mineral-laden water cascading over fallen rock left these shiny tiers of flowstone in the Big Room.

kept that way for posterity. There is great drama here. Can the cave be kept in good condition with the park as the vehicle? That was the theory . . . conserving the cave by developing it. A great paradox . . . requiring constant vigilance."

the temperature inside the cave remains close to 67°. To minimize the damaging effects of the dry outside air on the cave formations, air locks have been installed. If the formations lose their moisture, they stop growing.

Protective measures were devised to minimize human impact: Visitors entering the cave first pass through an air curtain that blows lint from their clothing; then they go through an area where mist forces any remaining lint against their clothing. Along the cave trails, special kick plates collect any foreign material that may track in on someone's shoes. Guides teach visitors not to touch anything since skin oils will halt a formation's growth.

These preservation efforts prompted Tufts to say: "What is the key point about Kartchner? Not that it is beautiful nor that it will spur growth in Benson, but the fact that it is in excellent condition and is being

Kartchner Caverns State Park® offers two tours to the public. The year-round Rotunda/Throne Room tour covers about a half mile and lasts about 90 minutes. The Big Room tour — not available from about mid-April to mid-October when it is occupied by a bat colony, also wends over about a half mile, but takes about 15 minutes longer. State Parks personnel strongly urge people to make tour reservations by calling (520) 586-CAVE (2283).

The park, which has hiking trails and day-use and camping facilities, is open seven days a week, 7:30 A.M. to 6 P.M. It is located on State Route 90, nine miles south of Interstate 10 (Exit 302).